CW01512247

Avrom has given us a gift from his he
of simple and yet profound is hono:
with how Avrom has integrated so
professional life into these poems. His role as a therapist and a teacher
flow well with his years as a student of Buddhism and teacher of the
Gurdjieff Work. The range of this work from the seemingly mundane
aspects of everyday life to his reflections on life and death. These works
are to be savored and embodied. I thank you for this work.
    —Allen Koehn, D. Min., Professor Emeritus in Counseling
    Psychology at Pacifica Graduate Institute, and author of *Dancing*
    At The Threshold.

Words can't be trusted. Language often warps and wraps up reality in a
neat box with a pretty ribbon on top confirming deeply held assumptions.
What to make of deceptively simple arrangements of syllables that
delight, confound and bend us toward deeper understanding of our
authentic inner selves and the mysterious universe that surrounds us?
This is the exciting journey that Avrom Altman's "haiku eye" casts for
the reader in this vibrant collection of blissful syllabic flowers.
    —Morrie Warshawski, author of *this afternoon*, *Out of Nowhere*, and
    Shaking the Money Tree.

We've come to expect brevity, wisdom and wit from haiku poetry
and *Flowers of Emptiness: Imaginal Haiku* provides a treasure trove of these
qualities ranging from humor to hard-won insight. Throughout the
volume we are aware of a deeply intelligent mind thoughtfully viewing
the world and his place in it. The subjects range from Zen illuminations
to nature, love, memory, nostalgia, aging, grief and death. Always with
a light touch and a great deal of heart, his honest pondering into the
human condition is often illuminated by humor. Read these vital haiku
aloud, slowly, taking a deep breath in between. Enjoy.
    —Kimberley Snow, author of *In Buddha's Kitchen.*

Flowers of Emptiness

Imaginal Haiku

BY

Avrom Altman

SUNGOLD EDITIONS • SANTA BARBARA, CALIFORNIA
2023

This book is dedicated to
my maternal grandmother Rose,
mother Claire, partner in life and love Rachel,
daughter Rebekah, and granddaughters
Alia and Iris

and to

my friend and mentor Barry Spacks,
the first poet laureate of Santa Barbara,
who unfailingly inspired and encouraged me.

"At this moment only does my life exist."

Dōgen

(Founder of the Soto school of Zen Buddhism in Japan)

The Nature of Haiku

In the summer of 1971, my friend Jack and I lived in tents at China Camp near the Tassajara Zen Mountain Monastery. We were sitting zazen and attending lectures by Shunryū Suzuki Roshi. Except when we were soaking in the hot springs up the trail above the zendo. It was heaven. A sometimes arduous heaven. Sitting zazen facing the wall is a daunting endeavor. Sometimes it goes well. Sometimes body and mind squirm until the bell rings. But being in the presence of Suzuki Roshi and the other students provided invisible support. And listening to Suzuki Roshi was invaluable. When giving a talk and answering questions, he had a way of pointing out fallacies in thinking, or taking the wind out of the sails of egoism, or pointing to a new way of seeing.

After the summer, I returned to Washington University in St. Louis and, while enrolled in Donald Finkel's poetry course, discovered H.G. Henderson's *An Introduction to Haiku*. The haiku were resonant with what I was learning about Zen Buddhism. Roshi said, "When a bird sings, the calmness of the mountain, more than when you did not hear any sound." How like a haiku! It's not surprising that R. H. Blythe wrote "Haiku is a form of Zen." Both inner and outer circumstances need to be just so for a haiku to flower—to bloom from contact with both the moment and the ground from which the moment emerges. In Chapter 43 of his seminal work, *Shōbōgenzō*, Dōgen interpreted the

Japanese kanji *kūge* (空華) as *flowers of emptiness* meaning both an enlightened state and that all things in the world are the cosmic *flowering of emptiness*. Here again the affinity between haiku and Zen is evident. Haiku resonate with the energy of the liminal as form arises from emptiness and emptiness permeates all form.

When a haiku blooms, I experience an unusual feeling in my chest—a tincture of blended recognition and poignancy. In *Haiku and Zen: The Bodhisattva of Forgetfulness*, Brian Tasker wrote that the Japanese term *yūgen* (幽玄) "conveys ineffable mystery and ... might be described as something that moves us deeply without us quite knowing why." This requires a receptivity and inner listening not common when distracted by inner chatter or busy with daily tasks. I recommend taking your time—as if slowing down time itself—when reading haiku. Let them drop like a stone into the pool of who you are. Psyche will let you know if there is an instant of recognition that blooms in your inner mirror. Saitō Sanki described this as "the opening of his haiku eye."

Below is a brief, condensed history of haiku intended to enhance your engagement with and appreciation of the haiku you find here. My humble hope is that somewhere in the leaves of the tree of this book your own *haiku eye* will open—either for the first time or happily again—and meet mine.

空華

Haiku are a unique form of poetic expression. Though religious experience has been the subject of poetry for centuries, haiku are not religious. Rather, they attempt to relate singular moments fully. This evocation of the vibrancy of a moment, emergent yet transient, beckons to the inner ear tuned to the invisible sound of now. Haiku speak across religious and cultural boundaries and are recognizable as an expression of quintessential human experience.

Haiku began as an element of an oral poetic form called renga and developed in the milieu of Japanese court life. Elevated to a literary art in the fourteenth century by Nijō Yoshimoto, renga are comprised of a *call* from one poet of 17 sound units constructed in short phrases of 5, 7, 5 (often thought of as 17 syllables, though a syllable can have more than one Japanese sound unit) followed by the *response* of another poet in the form of sound units of 7, 7. This could be repeated 50 times making a total of one hundred stanzas. Remarkably, the first 7 of each *response* replies to the preceding 5, 7, 5, yet the second 7 of the same *response* is free to set off in a new direction. In this way, renga are like a conversation with many twists. They continually surprise.

Hokku, which were the opening *call* of 17 sound units and later came to be called haikai and then haiku, broke away from renga in the 1670s. This new style was mastered by Matsuo Bashō while he lived in Edo (now Tokyo). He subsequently traveled throughout Japan and his experiences became the subject of his haiku. Bashō was followed by Yosa Buson, Kobayashi Issa, Masaoka Shiki and others in a lineage of countless descendants and branching streams.

It is a common misconception that haiku have a fixed format and are delimited with regard to subject matter and poetic range of expression. Historically, once hokku (haiku) became a poetic form distinct from renga, which was circumscribed with regard to form and function, it was free to develop in new and often surprising ways. This led to lively arguments and debates spanning centuries and continuing to this day relating to the lineation and number of syllables in haiku; if haiku should be humorous or serious; must reference season and nature or not; should *read* as if written or spoken; should have rhythmical breaks or can have syntactical breaks; should be simple and direct or should have philosophical import; should be grounded and concrete or can be imaginal and inclusive of the reflexivity of the poet. Additionally, as noted by Henderson, it is important to keep in mind that Japanese does not use articles, prepositions, pronouns, distinctions between singular and plural, or indications of gender in the manner used in English.

The Japanese language shaped haiku and influenced translations of Japanese haiku which either struggled to adhere to the imagined original intent of the poet or struggled to modify the intent of the poet in the language of the translator. As Benjamin Whorf indicated in *Language, Thought and Reality*, all languages bestow gifts of perspective but also circumscribe what we can experience. It is hard to articulate—even have—an experience for which there are no words. In 1999, Hiroaki Sato wrote, "Today it may be possible to describe haiku but not to define it." The distance between the conventional haiku of Bashō, the *life-exploring school* of haiku of Ishida Hakyō, the contemporary or *gendai haiku* of Kaneko Tōta, the *Newly Rising Haiku* of Saitō Sanki, the *new art haiku* of Shishū, the *anti-traditionalist haiku* of Katō Ikuya, and the recent haiku incorporating disjunctive technique of Nicholas Virgilio is vast.

Some find it disconcerting that the parameters determining the structure of haiku are not fixed. This was true hundreds of years ago and continues to be a subject of debate, dispute and disagreement among those who create haiku and those who appreciate haiku. On this subject, Marlene Mountain wrote, "My current definition of haiku is that haiku can no longer be defined." Witness the divergence of form and style in the conflicting philosophical and editorial positions of current publications such as *Modern Haiku* and *Frogpond*. Yet there is common ground and source from which haiku arise. Richard Gilbert wrote that haiku "penetrate to the deeper layers of identity and self, providing a glimpse of the ground of poetic being." As such, haiku are expressions of each poet's immersion in and transmission of a unique and ephemeral yet eternal instant. They employ simplicity, surprise, and reversal of expectation. These elements challenge literal interpretation and engage the active re-authoring of the poem by the reader. In *Zen and Japanese Culture*, Daisetz Suzuki wrote that "a haiku does not express ideas but . . . puts forward images reflecting intuitions. These intuitions are not figurative representations made use of by the poetic mind, but they directly point to intuitions, indeed, are intuitions themselves."

Poetry is an invitation. We are invited to enter the mysterious nature of creativity in which the distinction between the seer and the seen is a thin veil. The invitation is to become responsive to joining the poet in the moment of creation. This requires a relaxation of discursive thinking and the objectification of perceived impressions. Instead, one opens to *resonance*, to the echo in oneself of that which moved the poet. James Hillman wrote that the ground of psychic life is not literal and "the most fecund approach to the study of mind is through its highest imaginal responses." As readers of haiku, we are challenged to accept that haiku are shaped by the culture, language and what Henri Corbin called the *mundis imaginalis* or the inner imaginal world of each poet and reader. The haiku embodies and the reader discovers a poetic and metaphoric image that is firmly grounded yet also a mystery. The mysterious element is sometimes related to the lack of a clearly stated locus of experience which gives the impression of an *absence*. It is also related to the reflexivity of the poet which evokes the reflexivity of the reader and allows for direct and unexpected experience of the poem. The reader is invited to be receptive to their own intuition and emergent presence as essential, co-occurring components of the revealed. This gives you the opportunity to *re-author* the haiku in an instant Henderson referred to as *illumination*. Japanese haiku poet Katō Ikuya called this the "asphyxial condition of being moved."

May it be so!

With this in mind and heart, I offer this collection of
haiku with humble awareness of my own limitations and
invite your intuition to help bring the haiku to life.

Flowers of Emptiness

Imaginal Haiku

this garment of life
our most treasured possession
stitched from emptiness

just sitting
in this old garment of tears
still flirting with bliss

breath still
body and mind fall away
how full my heart is!

sudden surprise!
silent illumination
by being embraced

illumination
the flower of emptiness
flower of itself

空華

wind on Ruby Lake
words scatter and sink from view
no haiku for you!

wind ripples Rock Lake
sudden aspen susurrus
stillness in motion

cry of hawk
sharp squeal of rabbit
swallowed by silence

sunset at tree line
stillness fills this empty bowl
nothing changes shape

atop a zafu
my breath stops a lark
tumbles off its perch

my eyes
in the sky
in the pond

a school of ghost koi
glowing in the night pond
the moon

sitting by the spring
water rises from stone
old face wet with tears

sitting by the spring
zafu round like silence
mind sound as light

空華

gazing into your eyes
my heart begins to miss you
even love is dew!

my heart offers tea
love steeped in secrets and lies
we swallow and bow

breathing the unknown
in the winter of our lives
we sip shared air

I lie where she lies
both breathless with a poem
only our hearts knew

remembered moments
lustrous as a string of pearls
on an aging thread

空華

I found my glasses
but the path is slick as lies
I'll sit and then nap

lost on the path
sitting on a log to rest
what took me so long

thinking twice I trip
children laugh and sit with me
patting my old head

atop a zafu
old ears ringing
I miss the silence!

how foolish
arduous trek to return
having never left

I don't fear thieves
they steal only what I hold
not what holds me

I lost my glasses
my old eyes can't see the path
still the Way is clear

空華

I am old and slow
children pick my pockets clean
soon birds will my bones

clouds float in both eyes
cicadas whine in both ears
still I flirt with bliss

through my daughter's eyes
our ancestors see beyond
my place on the path

the mirror
the mirror
makes of the room

after a long soak
an old man in the mirror
stares back right at me

wonder that is now
that is past that is next
kensho or old age?

I'm an old man
rattling bones wrinkled skin
and astonished heart!

空華

my old friend is ill
the path once lined with blossoms
now hip deep with snow

my friend is dying
precious insignificance
dust made of wonder

my friend is dying
yet jokes about my distress
each life a koan

my old friend's eyes fade
the path at his own tree line
slowly vanishes

my friend is dying
prepared to drop this garment
I make rice for one

dying he whispered
we're morning dew in the light
of a mystery

last breath
my old friend beside me
as still as Buddha

my old friend is dead
in daylight we fought and laughed
in moonlight ashes

when a friend departs
what is the half-life of grief?
I too seem a ghost

I can't find my friend
his body on the pyre
his unique flair, where?

my dear friend is dead
the scoundrel left me behind
who is the ghost now?

空華

spring blossoms falling
I wear time as a smile
petals as a robe

flesh and bones
know the unknown remains
we're ghosts blessed with breath

old men bet quarters
hold hands and ponder the odds
two chairs are empty

petals on the path
radiance returned to soil
as are you and I

last breath at daybreak
my father's eyes illumined
with remembered light

ghosts rise in half-light
the moon flirts with the lake
each cloud a new death

deep in second sleep
dreaming of soul after death
we miss this swift gift

shades drawn by the path
that sun neither lights nor heats
ghosts cast no shadow

each tear a moon
lit by immanence within
a well of sorrow

ghosts seek us at dusk
flesh and blood no longer home
they weep within us

mist covers the stars
the moon falls out of the lake
as will we from life

空華

my robe is tattered
heart brimming with delight
call me the rich monk

each step hurts my feet
sitting zazen hurts my knees
call me lying monk

I squat near the path
sutras, begging bowl and robes
call me the fake monk

people don't see me
mind and belly empty
call me lucky monk

each moment is full
my begging bowl is empty
call me the fat monk

I dream of tresses
smooth skin beneath dresses
call me the bad monk

each moment at sea
each port lined with pyres
call me the true monk

空華

sitting on the sill
neither inside nor outside
sweeping thoughts like dust

what first mind reflects
each empty mirror reveals
our face before birth

a toddler scampers
out of sight
the unknown

I wander this maze
each day a warren of sighs
pregnant with wonder

what is right practice
the target seeks your arrow
aim and let go

sitting in silence
unexpected resonance
rings this empty bell!

skirt of the unseen
silence teases my old mind
still, I flirt with bliss

illumination
shimmering in all things
I too am a sail

sky full of lake light
life of long grief and brief bliss
heart of gratitude

brief as shooting stars
we are wonder arising
dust lit from within

awareness

out of blood and breath

out of itself

lush as a ripe fig
letting slip the knots of life
my heart splits open

here then swept away
this illuminated dust
that is briefly us

an old monk just died
dropping body like a robe
on illusion's floor

light pools on the path
moonrise over Mount Jiri
words obscure the Way

like fish in a stream
all in this floating world
slips away

full cup
equal parts beauty and loss
perfect tea

Human Nature and Haiku

Cold cliffs, more beautiful the deeper you enter ‑
Yet no one travels this road.
White clouds idle about the tall crags;
On the green peak a single monkey wails.
What other companions do I need?
I grow old doing as I please.
Though face and form alter with the years,
I hold fast to the pearl of the mind.

Hánshān
(Chinese Zen recluse, *Cold Mountain*, tr. Burton Watson)

Haiku are direct yet tease the imaginal inner life of the reader. They arise from the essential *pearl of the mind.* James Hillman wrote, "Imaging means releasing events from their literal understanding...in order to search out their metaphorical significances for the soul." He proposed that mind is fundamentally poetic and metaphoric in nature. Drawing on the work of Hillman, Peter Willis referred to *imaginal reflection, imaginal knowing, awareness knowing,* and *evoked awakeness.*

Anchored yet free, haiku have clear form but address emptiness. Richard Gilbert wrote, "Haiku achieve a powerful contextual paradox regarding ground and groundlessness, space and spacelessness, time and the timeless, the real and the imaginal, figure and ground." They convey a moment's essence yet accent transience related to the Japanese term *mono no aware* (物の哀れ) which reflects a sensitivity to, awareness of, and empathy for the impermanence of things. A revealed, emergent core and expression of each fleeting moment is the heart of haiku. Each arises from direct expression of the essence of nature and human nature unmediated yet informed by blemishes in the mirror of awareness. The reader is invited to intuit—to imaginally embody—the unconditioned, immanent *I-Amness* of each moment—to savor the flowers of emptiness.

空華

For a man to attain enlightenment is like the moon lodging in the water. The moon does not get wet, the water does not break. The moon, though it is light is wide and large, lodges in the slightest bit of water. The entire moon, the whole sky, lodges in a dewdrop on the grass, lodges in a drop of water. Enlightenment does not break a man as the moon does not pierce the water.

Dōgen

空華

jō akete
tsuki sashireyo
ukimidō

open the lock
let the moon shine in -
Floating Temple

Bashō

81

Sources

默照禅

silent illumination
emergent
reflexive awareness
luminous
immanent presence
vibration
within
stillness

stillness
within
vibration
immanent presence
luminous
reflexive awareness
emergent
silent illumination

by A. Altman

默照禅: Japanese for *silent illumination zen* or *meditation*. Also translated as *shikantaza* derived from the Chinese term 默照禅 (mo-chao) for zazen or *serene reflection*, itself derived from the Sanskrit term *utkuṭuka-stha* or *samatha* and *vipaśyanā*, the two basic forms of Buddhist meditation.

शून्यता

In the *Lotus Sutra*, a union between *emptiness*, the so-called negative teaching of the *Prajnaparamita* (usually translated as *The Perfection of Wisdom*, the key text of Mahāyāna Buddhism), and the positive identity of essences, an understanding that the thusness of all things is a meeting between emptiness and form—an *illuminated emptiness*.

This *emptiness* can be discovered in a maximally open state of awareness attainable through meditation.

शून्यता: *Emptiness* in Sanskrit

आनन्द शरीर

The *bliss body* is the junction between formless Source and form. It is the place where consciousness and energy meet and intermingle; a space of abiding stillness and perfect contentment without cause or reason. The experience of love at the *bliss body* is not emotional ecstasy, which has an opposite, but rather is a spontaneous opening of the heart experienced as a sense of purest silent joy.

The *bliss body* is the reflected light of Source. Its only difference from Source is that it contains a sense of individuality or *I Am-ness*—pure beingness.

First outlined in the *Taittiriya Upanishad*, the *bliss body* is one of the *koshas*, literally translated as "house" or "sheath" which map the process of embodiment from unmanifest, undifferentiated potential (the ocean) into the physical form of the body (the wave).

आनन्द शरीर: Sanskrit for *bliss body*.

About the Author

Avrom Altman began studying Zen Buddhism in 1967 and sat zazen with Shunryū Suzuki Roshi at the Tassajara Zen Mountain Center. In 1972, Avrom attended a ten-month residential course at Sherborne House under the direction of J.G. Bennett, a student of G.I. Gurdjieff. In the 1980s, while a resident of Claymont, an intentional community created by Bennett, Avrom was head gardener, Gurdjieff Movements teacher, and directed studies of ten-month residential courses before becoming President of the Claymont Society for Continuous Education. He became a Mevlevi semazen and participated in the Sema under the guidance of sheiks Suleiman Dede and Jelaludin Loras. Avrom is a member of the Board of Directors of the Gurdjieff Heritage Society and has led groups and over 100 seminars and retreats based on the Gurdjieff Work and Gurdjieff Movements.

Avrom is Professor Emeritus at Pacifica Graduate Institute where he served as Director of Research, Associate Chair, and Academic Senate President. He received the Distinguished Service Award in 2009 and the Award for Extraordinary Accomplishments as Soul Tender in the World in 2015. Avrom is a Licensed Professional Counselor, Licensed Marriage and Family Therapist, Certified Hakomi Therapist, and has been in private practice for over 40 years.

He is a member of the CIVIQ Society, founder of the activist group Rise Up for Justice, co-founder of Flip Nation and its 50 state groups, administrator of Equal and its nine regional groups, and administrator of Just Policy Action.

Avrom lives with Rachel, his wife of over 50 years, in Santa Barbara, California. They have a daughter, Rebekah, and two granddaughters, Alia and Iris.

Flowers of Emptiness: Imaginal Haiku is Avrom's first published book of haiku.

CPSIA information can be obtained
at www.ICGtesting.com
Printed in the USA
BVHW032244291222
655301BV00001B/92